Miss Lizzy's Story

By Charles H. Knight

Annotated by Ersula K. Odom

Copyright © Ersula K. Odom 2020. All rights reserved. This book may not be reproduced in whole or in part without written permission from the publisher, except by a reviewer who may quote brief passages in a review; nor may any part of this book be reproduced, stored in retrieval system, or transmitted in any form or by any means, electronic, mechanical, photocopying, recording, or other, without prior written permission from Sula Too LLC.

ISBN-13: 978-1-7339542-8-0 Paperback
ISBN   978-1-7339542-4-2 ebook
Library of Congress Control Number:2019957608

Printed and bound in the United States of America January 2020
Cover photo : Library of Congress, Prints & Photographs Division, FSA/OWI Collection, [reproduction number, e.g., LC-USF34-9058-C]

Edited by Carol A. Page

Annotated by Ersula K. Odom

Published by Guiding Knight Press
A production of Sula Too LLC Tampa, Florida
www.sulatoo.com/guidingknight

Miss Lizzy's Story

By Charles H. Knight

Annotated by Ersula K. Odom

Guiding Knight Press
A Production of Sula Too LLC
Tampa Florida

About the Cover:

The artwork found on the cover was created by Charles H. Knight. He was an artist in a true sense as he produced both literary and visual art. He wrote narrative, poetry and illustrated his visions.

Presenting his art and poetry will be a feature you can look forward to in this and future publications of Mr. Knight's work.

The black and white photograph is courtesy of the Library of Congress.

Table of Contents

Dreams	**6**
Above The Trees	**9**
Great Depression	**14**
Black Sharecroppers	**16**
Canning	**18**
W. A. Pattillo' High School	**26**
Segregated Schools Ruling	**28**
If I Can	**36**
Good Bye Auntie	**44**

The Guiding Knight Series

Guiding Knight Press Editions, published by Sula Too Press, bring to you the writings of Charles Howard Knight and/or those individuals believed to be related to him.

This first book was inspired by Geneva Kimber Knight's desire to preserve and protect the legacy of her late husband and friend.

Mr. Knight spent a lifetime writing and dreaming of being published. This is the first of several books inspired by and designed to continue his dream.

Miss Lizzy's Story

Dreams

by Ersula K. Odom

Dreams vanish

When hopes fade

Like clouds

Many shapes are made

Dreams vanish

If not captured

If not shared

If not nurtured

Dreams come to life

At the sound of hope

When hope speaks loudly

Dreams and Hope elope

Charles H. Knight

Courtesy of Charles G. Knight

Miss Lizzy's Story

Above The Trees

Above the trees there's a misty haze,
    Below in the meadow a few cattle graze;
The birds overhead keep circling around,
    Occasionally landing to see what's to be found;
A Little turtle moves slowly by,
    The grasshopper leaping with springs very high.

Over the slopes on top of the hill,
    Stands the master bull,
      watching the herd get their fill;
There goes the honey bee moving along,
    Heading for a bee hive, a thousand strong;
Over there is a spider spinning a web,
    Not too big, not too small,
Just large enough to hold what falls.

There is a pine stretching high,
    Endlessly toward the sky;
There's a robin, spreading his wing,
    Here come the blue jay doing his thing.
I often wonder what they are so busy doing
    In this beautiful hue;
Even the little ants keep busy
    The whole day through.

                        - Charles H. Knight

Charles H. Knight

How to read this story:

Read Miss Lizzy's uninterrupted story from beginning to end by reading only the odd pages.

Then reread, stopping along the way to read the associated sidebar pages on the even pages.

Miss Lizzy's Story

Charles H. Knight

Miss Lizzy's Story

One person who had a positive effect on so many lives, was this woman, Elizabeth Powell Bellamy. She opened doors and paved the way for many unfortunate men, women, and children to succeed in life - because she cared.

From the early nineteen thirties, until her demise in the mid-nineteen eighties, "Miss Lizzy" as she was called, made room and shelter for countless people in her home. Sharing a five room house with her husband and three daughters, didn't deter Miss Lizzy from making room for those who needed it.

Charles H. Knight

Great Depression

The Great Depression started in the United States after a major fall in stock prices that began around September 4, 1929, and became worldwide news with the stock market crash of October 29, 1929, (known as Black Tuesday). Between 1929 and 1932, worldwide gross domestic product (GDP) fell by an estimated 15%. By comparison, worldwide GDP fell by less than 1% from 2008 to 2009 during the Great Recession. Some economies started to recover by the mid-1930s. However, in many countries, the negative effects of the Great Depression lasted until the beginning of World War II. [1]

"*The problems of the Great Depression affected virtually every group of Americans. No group was harder hit than African Americans, however. By 1932, approximately half of black Americans were out of work. In some Northern cities, whites called for blacks to be fired from any jobs as long as there were whites out of work. Racial violence again became more common, especially in the South. Lynchings, which had declined to eight in 1932, surged to 28 in 1933.*" [2]

Miss Lizzy's Story

In the nineteen-thirties, she lost her oldest sister to death caused by child birth, leaving two small children to be cared for during the ***Great Depression.***

Lizzy, at the time had no children. Being young and energetic, she insisted on helping with her sister's young children, a boy and the newborn girl.

Elizabeth and Moses Bellamy had been married only a few years and she assumed the new experience of caring for the children would be good, caring for the young boy and new born girl. She nurtured them until it was safe for their father to take over and make a life for them.

Charles H. Knight

Black sharecroppers

"After the end of the American Civil War and the abolition of slavery, many African Americans and some whites in the rural South made a living by renting small plots of land from large landowners who were usually white and pledging a percentage of their crops to the landowners at harvest—a system known as sharecropping. Landowners provided sharecroppers with land, seeds, tools, clothing, and food. Charges for the supplies were deducted from the sharecroppers' portion of the harvest, leaving them with substantial debt to landowners in bad years. Sharecroppers would become caught in continual debt, especially during weak harvests or periods of low prices, such as when cotton prices fell in the 1880s and '90s. Once in debt, sharecroppers were forbidden by law to leave the landowner's property until their debt was paid, effectively putting them in a state of slavery to the landowner. Between 1880 and 1930 the proportion of Southern farms operated by the tenants increased from 36 to 55 percent." https://www.britannica.com/topic/debt-slavery#ref1223082

It wasn't just the "bad" years. The system was designed so that sharecroppers never got out of debt even when the harvests were good. No receipts were ever provided; the owners kept the "books" and they might let the sharecropper get a glance and even in those cases where the sharecroppers kept their own records, the records of the landowners prevailed.

Miss Lizzy's Story

Rural life was hard for ***Black sharecroppers*** who chose to earn their livelihood by tilling the soil of the "Good Earth", with little or no education, and often cheated out of their meager earnings made from the crops.

Charles H. Knight

The share cropping system may have been a response to the disproportionate skill advantage that a large number of blacks possessed as compared to the former slave masters who then had to sink or swim based on personal merit.

Canning:

According to Ball®, canning is just one step beyond cooking. Canning involves processing food in closed glass canning jars at high temperatures. The heat interrupts natural spoilage by destroying food contaminants and, at the same time, removes air from the jars. As the jars cool, a vacuum seal forms – to prevent recontamination.

Display of Home-Canned Food. [Between 1941 and 1945] Photograph. Retrieved from the Library of Congress, <www.loc.gov/item/2017878891/>.

Miss Lizzy's Story

However, Miss Lizzy was not a sharecropper, nor did she live in the rural area, but she knew how to grow vegetables and ***canned*** almost everything needed to survive the hard and very lean times. She fed the hungry, clothed and housed the homeless, whenever possible.

Shortly after her first child was born in nineteen thirty two, she lost another sister because of faulty childbirth. This time it was four boys ranging in ages, two to twelve years. Again Lizzy opened her heart, and home to make life a little easier for those motherless children. [EN2]

Charles H. Knight

Miss Lizzy's Story

Whatever the need was at the time, Miss Lizzy was always there to help fill a void in one's life.

It was urgent and almost a must for a father to remarry some woman so he would have help with his young children. In rural areas, few men, if any, knew very little about handling young babies. It was a woman's job and men didn't bother with the task of learning how. Until such time occurred, Miss Lizzy was the mother and cared for them as her own.

It seemed that crisis after crisis continued to crop up during her young married years. Another sister died in nineteen thirty four, leaving three small boys without a mother.

The loss was heartbreaking. All her sisters had died in such a short span of time for the

Charles H. Knight

Miss Lizzy's Story

same reason, childbirth.

No matter how sad she was over the loss, somehow she knew what had to be done. Even with a small girl of her own, Miss Lizzy knew room had to be made for those young boys until things got better.

After nineteen thirty seven, with three girls in her family, things changed for the better. All the males had found wives to mother and help care for the children involved. However, Miss Lizzy never brushed aside the need to help when necessary.

Education was a top priority on Lizzy's list. Because of the times, getting an education she and her sisters, seemed to be at the bottom of the list. She vowed it would not be the same with her children. They had to

Charles H. Knight

achieve a higher degree of education than the fifth grade she had completed.

In spite of difficulties, Miss Lizzy moved forward with the changing times. She refashioned clothes given to her for use by white people who knew her husband, Moses.

Necessity taught her how to make use of anything passed on to her. Miss Lizzy would take an old dress or pair of pants and turn it into something new for her husband as well as her children, creating her own style and design.

For years, both Black and White people trusted her alteration knowledge and skill. She was very good, and they knew it.

W. A. Pattillo' High School

Founded as the Tarboro Colored High School and was renamed in 1943 for W. A. Patillo, the school's first principal.

The first high school class graduated in 1924 with three members.*

An examination of Google Maps reveals that Miss Lizzy's house was less than a block away from the school. Therefore, the children in her home would only had to walk to the corner and cross the street.

*Source: Thy Noble Sons, Thy Daughters Fair by C. Rudolph Knight and Dr. Lawrence W. S. Auld.

Miss Lizzy's Story

Regardless of how fortunate and how successful Lizzy was, she always remained humble and steadfast in all that she did.

Early in the nineteen forties, she opened her doors to girls seeking a high school education.

The ***W. A. Pattillo' School*** was the only one in the area or county at which Black people could attain a much needed high school education. This was very important to Black people during the harsh time of segregation. The school offered an opportunity to those who were willing to come.

It was not a must for some young Black men to get a higher education because of much needed farm laborers. For the, girls, it was

Charles H. Knight

Segregated Schools Ruling

On May 17, 1954, U.S. Supreme Court Justice Earl Warren delivered the unanimous ruling in the landmark civil rights case Brown v. Board of Education of Topeka, Kansas. State-sanctioned segregation of public schools was a violation of the 14th amendment and was therefore unconstitutional. This historic decision marked the end of the "separate but equal" precedent set by the Supreme Court nearly 60 years earlier in Plessy v. Ferguson and served as a catalyst for the expanding civil rights movement during the decade of the 1950s.

Prior to this ruling Black students were subjected to studying from used books discarded by white schools and generally were not receiving equal access to educational materials.

It was important for girls to get an education to help avoid having to become a domestic worker and having to serve at the pleasure of an employer and sons. In spite of the lack of resources, Black students were excelling due to teachers like Miss Lizzy in many areas of the country. Currently there are countless monuments and buildings erected to honor students of this timeframe who succeeded by the hands of countless Miss Lizzys.

Miss Lizzy's Story

different. It was imperative for them to obtain a higher degree of learning, especially in the field of teaching.

So, Miss Lizzy insisted that the girls sharing her home along with her children, to acquire a high school education. They were required to study hard and without fail, get a Diploma.

One thing she did was to inform every parent, her rule would prevail while in her home - no exception.

When the Supreme Court ruled that ***segregated schools were unconstitutional***, Lizzy still continued her open-door policy for those needing a home away from home.

When segregated schools ended, however Lizzy moved into another phase of helping.

Charles H. Knight

Miss Lizzy's Story

She nourished and cared for the elderly; especially those needing personal attention.

Many elderly women lived out their last years, days and hours under the same roof with the Bellamys. Family members of some women didn't have the knowledge, patience nor stamina needed to give specialized attention.

Not only did Miss Lizzy care for those who needed her humble service, she also knew how and where to locate relatives and friends of almost everyone living in the surrounding rural areas.

The human grapevine was a vital way of comminication for those living in remote places. When something happened, be it illness, violence, marriage, or death, news

Charles H. Knight

traveled by word-of-mouth within a very short time.

As time permitted, Miss Lizzy's daughters graduated from high school and ventured to various parts of the country. She visited them periodically, to enhance her knowledge about other things and ways of life. She maintained contact over the years with those who passed through her door, remembering how important they were to her.

Nevertheless, time and age caught up with her. She realized life was not forever.

Even though failing health was taking its toll on her, she tried not to complain about her bad days when she was not feeling well.

Charles H. Knight

Miss Lizzy's Story

In the summer of nineteen eighty six, she said to me , "You're one nephew I can count on. Come home as often as you can, because I won't be here much longer." From time to time I'd ask, "How you feel?" She'd always say, "I'm doing the best I can."

This she had done, during her entire life, "The best she could," especially for those who needed someone. She was always there, with open arms, heart, love and compassion, giving of herself to the very end.

Charles H. Knight

If I Can

I asked if I can do it,
I was told that I can,

I promised never to stop
while I have these hands;

I'll stroke in the morning,
I'll stroke through the night,

I'll keep on and on in broad daylight.

Upon these walls,
I'll sign my name,

On countless sheets of paper,
I'll do the same;

I asked you to help me,
so don't let me down,

Now that I've started, I won't turn around.

Miss Lizzy's Story

Don't get discouraged,
just keep the faith,

It may come soon,
but not too late

To enter every home in the state;
Why do you fret when I'm not together?
For when I'm right,
I know I can do better.

I'll touch every heart
in every home some day,

I feel sure now and I know
that I can someday warm

The hearts of many
over this beautiful land,

Just because I asked, 'If I Can.'

- Charles H. Knight

End Note 1

Miss Lizzy Was A Real Person

1930 Census lists:
Howard Powell head
Lucy Powell-1873 wife
    Moses Bellamy-1906 son-in-law
    Elizabeth Bellamy-1910 *daughter*
    Robert Bellamy- boarder
    Daisy Bellamy boarder

Miss Lizzy's Story

1930 Census also lists:

on the same page:
Abram Bellamy	Head
Bridga Bellamy	wife
Joe Knight	son-in-law

on the same page:
Dock Knight	head
Ruthie Knight	wife
Maggie	granddaughter
Marion Knight	grandson
George Knight	grandson
Ethel Lloyd	grandaughter
Lossie Deale	daughter

Charles H. Knight

This photo of a North Carolina family near Raligh was found in the LOC archives. Amazingly it closely match the number and make up of Miss Lizzy's household. Four nephews from two to twelve, three nieces, her husband Moses and their own daughter.

Life is so strange that someday, someone may find that this is indeed Miss Lizzy.

Miss Lizzy's Story

End Note 2

"Shortly after her first child was born in nineteen thirty two, she lost another sister because of faulty childbirth. This time it was four boys, very young, ranging in ages, two to twelve years. Again Lizzy opened her heart, and home to make life a little easier for those motherless children."

Shown here is what was listed in the census records. The actual birth years often don't appear. Charles' delayed birth certificate records his year of birth as 1925.

1902 -1932 Susan Powell Knight

Sons in 1932:

> William, (1921)
> Charles (1926),
> Robert (1928)
> Albert (1932)

Charles H. Knight

Good Bye Auntie

They say the sons
Suffer for the sins
Of the father

I now know that
Daughters are protected
By the graces
Of the mother

Your smile and good will
created a desire for all
to protect that you cherished

Your love ones
Your memories
Your legacy

Your child is protected
By the sweet words
That others whisper to her

Your memory is protected
By the joy that we feel
As we see you in our mind's eye
As we speak warmly of you

Miss Lizzy's Story

Your legacy lives in the nieces
Who promises to be like you
 for the rest of their lives

Even in your pain the nurses said:
She's funny She's sweet
The doctors exhausted their powers to save you
For they knew you were special

But, you asked God to
hold your hand and he did

For he knew best &
He led you home to rest

by Ersula K. Odom

Charles H. Knight

Geneva Kimber Knight
Wife and guardian of C. H. Knight's legacy.

Ersula K Odom
CEO of Sula Too LLC, author, historian and publisher

Miss Lizzy's Story

About the Author

Charles Howard Knight, a Tarboro, North Carolina native attended W. A. Patillo School. After serving in the U.S. Navy during World War II, he furthered his education at the Robert Louis Stephenson School in New York City, and the Brown and Hofler School of Business in Brooklyn, New York.

Knight began writing in 1944 to 1947 while he was in the U.S. Navy. He primarily wrote short stories about military life but none of this work was published.

ALSO BY CHARLES H. KNIGHT

What Happened to Miss Emma
Walk Again By Faith

ALSO BY ERSULA K. ODOM

At Sula's Feet
Doris Ross Reddick
African Americans of Tampa

Miss Lizzy's Story

After becoming a life insurance underwriter for North Carolina Mutual Insurance Company, living in Reidsville, North Carolina, Knight couldn't find time to write.

Then, in 1970, Knight began again - this time penning poetry. He was relentless in his dedication to writing and ultimately realizing his dream with the release of his first book - "What Happened to Miss Emma."

Mr. Knight past away in 1996, leaving several manuscripts in various stages of development.

Charles H. Knight

Endnotes

*1 https://en.wikipedia.org/w/index.
php?title=Special:Book&bookcmd=book_
creator&referer=Great+Depression*

*2 Library of Congress - http://www.loc.gov/teachers/
classroommaterials/presentationsandactivities/presentations/
timeline/*

Miss Lizzy's Story

www.ingramcontent.com/pod-product-compliance
Lightning Source LLC
Chambersburg PA
CBHW071038080526
44587CB00015B/2670